D1716629

Welcome to the
Tree Stump

by Alix Wood

Ruby Tuesday Books

Published in 2024 by Ruby Tuesday Books Ltd.

Editor: Ruth Owen

Design and Production: Alix Wood

Photo credits
Alamy: 22R (Steve Holroyd), 25 (Malcolm Schuyl), 28B (Dorling Kindersley Ltd); Nature Picture Library: 7B (Stephen Dalton), 8 (Brent Stephenson), 9L (Jose Luis Gomez de Francisco), 17 (Mitsuhiko Imamori), 19T (Wild Wonders of Europe), 22L (Robert Thompson), 23 (Duncan McEwan), 27B (Laurie Campbell), 28T (Flip de Nooyer); Science Photo Library: 6BL (Eye of Science), 21T (Eye of Science); Shutterstock: Cover (Aleksander Bolbot/Chris Moody), 2–3, 4 (Aleksander Bolbot), 5TL (Bildagentur Zoonar GmbH), 5TR (Matti Salminen), 5B (Octavian Lazar), 6 (Yevhenii Chulovskyi), 7T (Stephan Morris), 8R (Photobox_gkr), 9R (Hanna Knutsson), 10L (nkula), 12 (Daykiney), 13TL (Ann Yuni), 13BL (Elena Fox), 13R (perlphoto), 14 (Oleh Liubimtsev), 15T (Peddalanka Ramesh Babu), 15B (Oleh Liubimtsev), 16T (Anne Coatesy), 16BL (David Dohnal), 16BC (Henrik Larsson), 16BR (Steve Midgley), 18L (Carl McKie), 18R (Sleepyhobbit), 19B (Petr Simon), 20 (Richard Hood), 24L (Daykiney), 24R (Martin Fowler), 26B (Beneda Miroslav), 27T (xpixel), 29 (Stephan Morris), 30–31; Superstock: 10R (J&C Sohns/Tier und Naturfotografie), 11 (Stephen Dalton), 26T (Thiebaud).

Library of Congress Control Number: 2023902801
Print (Hardback) ISBN 978-1-78856-295-9
Print (Paperback) ISBN 978-1-78856-296-6
eBook PDF ISBN 978-1-78856-297-3
ePub ISBN 978-1-78856-298-0

Published in Minneapolis, MN
Printed in the United States
www.rubytuesdaybooks.com

Contents

Words shown in **bold** in the text are explained in the glossary.

Welcome to the Tree Stump

Who and what lives in and around a tree stump?

The remains of an old oak tree can be home to many different living things.

A tree stump is a type of ecosystem. An ecosystem includes all the living things in an area. It also includes non-living things such as water, soil, and sunlight. Everything in an ecosystem has its own part to play.

Moss

Ants, beetles, **fungi**, and moss make the tree stump their home.

Ant

Female stag beetle

The animals and plants get what they need to live from this **microhabitat**.

Fungi

Let's find out what happens in this habitat.
Welcome to the tree stump!

A Slow Lunch

Two tentacles slowly feel their way over the tree stump.

The snail stops to munch on moss and leaves.

A snail has a tongue called a radula. The tongue is covered with about 12,000 tiny teeth!

Tentacle

Snail

Teeth on a snail's tongue

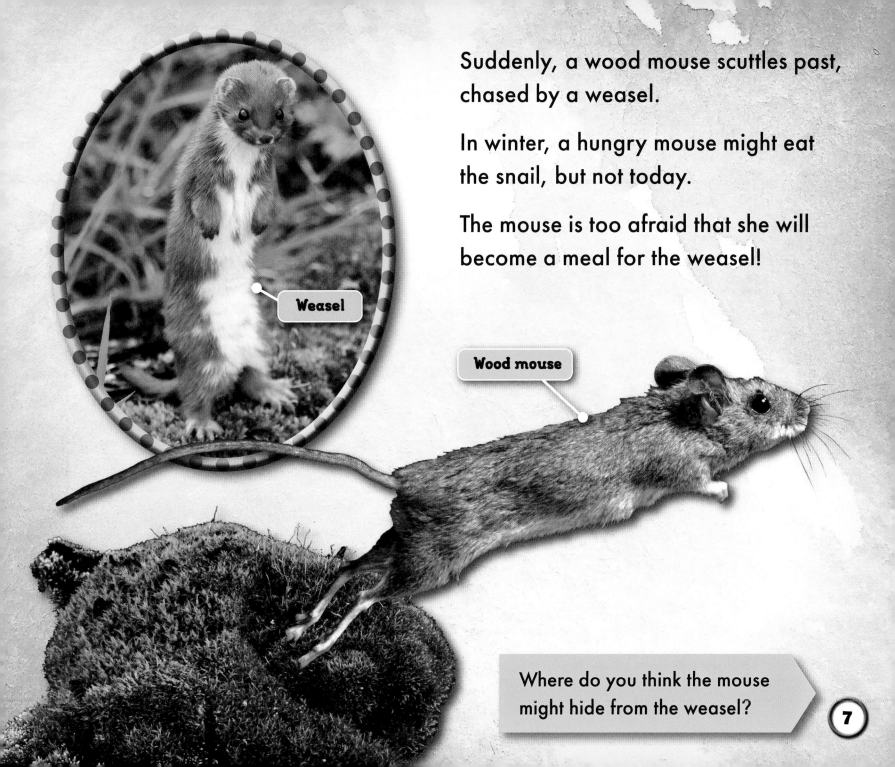

Suddenly, a wood mouse scuttles past, chased by a weasel.

In winter, a hungry mouse might eat the snail, but not today.

The mouse is too afraid that she will become a meal for the weasel!

Weasel

Wood mouse

Where do you think the mouse might hide from the weasel?

A Food Store

The wood mouse knows this tree stump well. She quickly hides in her burrow in the tree roots.

Wood mouse

Empty nut shells in the store cupboard

She scurries past her store cupboard that is full of nuts, seeds, and fungi.

Wood mice have a big appetite. They like to eat around 20 meals a day! So, they need to live close to a good source of food.

Next to the store, the mouse built a warm nest lined with leaves, moss, and grass.

She has four babies in the nest.

Baby wood mice

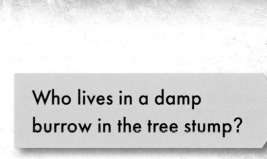

Who lives in a damp burrow in the tree stump?

A Friendly Neighbor

The wood mouse has some friendly neighbors.

A toad lives in a damp hole under the tree stump.

It's the perfect home because he needs to stay cool and moist.

Toad

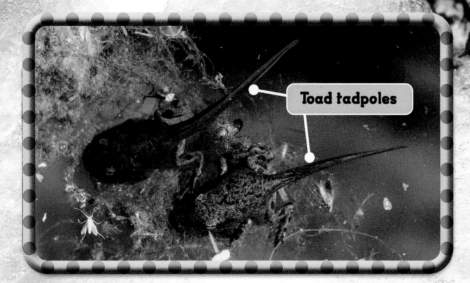

Toad tadpoles

The toad started life as an egg in a pond by the tree stump. He hatched into a tadpole. Once his four legs grew, he left the water to live on land.

At night, the toad goes hunting around the tree stump.

He catches worms, slugs, and insects with his long, sticky tongue.

Tongue

Worm

What plants help hide the toad and keep him cool and damp?

A Green Carpet

The old tree stump is covered with moss.

These tiny plants grow close together—they look like a springy, green carpet.

Mosses cling to tree bark and rocks with tiny hair-like parts called rhizoids.

Moss plant

Moss plants don't have roots for taking in water and nutrients. Instead, the whole tiny plant soaks up these things, a little like a sponge.

Fern plants also make their home on and around the tree stump.

A fern's featherlike fronds, or leaves, are tightly curled when they first sprout.

Fern fronds

New fern fronds

Unfurling fronds

As they grow, the fronds unfurl.

Ferns and mosses have been around since before the dinosaurs walked on Earth!

Could any animal be so small that it lives in the carpet of moss?

Tree Stump Superheroes

The moss is home to hundreds of tiny, fat superheroes—the almost indestructible moss piglets, or tardigrades.

These **microscopic** animals are smaller than a pencil dot!

They live in tiny amounts of water and suck juices from the moss.

Tardigrade

If the moss dries up, so do the tardigrades.

They go into a deep sleep and can stay this way for many years.

When it rains and the moss gets wet again, the tardigrades take in water and start moving around.

A dried-up tardigrade

Scientists sent some tardigrades into space on the outside of a spacecraft. They survived with no air and in super-cold temperatures. These tiny superheroes have also survived being boiled and crushed!

What other minibeasts are keeping moist under the moss?

A Damp Hiding Place

A bird lands on the tree stump and pecks up some moss.

The centipedes and woodlice hiding under the moss scurry away.

The centipedes were hunting for insects, spiders, and woodlice.

Blue tit

Centipede

Luckily, the bird isn't searching for a snack today. It wants the moss to line its nest.

Woodlouse

Pouch

Woodlouse

Eggs

A female woodlouse lays eggs into a pouch under her body. After the young hatch and leave her pouch, the mother stays close to the little woodlice for a few months.

Mother woodlouse

The woodlice on the tree stump feed on rotting wood, **leaf litter**, fungi, dead animals, and even poop!

Young woodlouse

Which beetle with huge antlers has been living under the tree stump for six years?

Meet a Stag Beetle

A male stag beetle digs his way out from under the tree stump.

He started his life as an egg, laid by a female beetle in the soil beneath the stump.

Male stag beetle

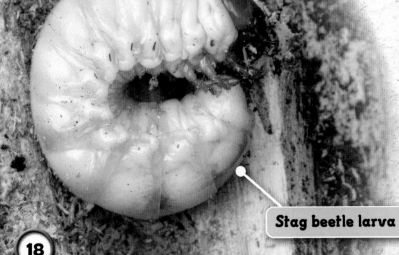

Stag beetle larva

He hatched from his egg as a fat **larva** and spent six years feeding on rotting wood.

Then one day, the larva made a **cocoon** from soil and wood.

Inside the cocoon he went through lots of changes to become an adult beetle.

Stag beetle cocoon

Jaws

Fighting stag beetles

The stag beetle is the size of an adult human's thumb. He will use his antler-like jaws to fight over females with other male stag beetles.

Which tree stump resident looks like a plant, but isn't?

Colorful Lichens

Lots of colorful lichens grow on the tree stump's bark.

A lichen looks like a plant, but it's actually made of two living things.

It is a partnership between a fungus and **algae**.

All the colors on this bark are different lichens.

A lichen's main body is made of fungus that attaches the lichen to the tree stump's bark.

This close-up picture of a lichen was taken by a powerful microscope.

Algae

Fungus

Birds and squirrels use lichen to build their nests, and it's a tasty treat for a wood mouse.

The fungus gives the algae shelter.

In exchange, the algae make sugary food that they share with the fungus.

What flying insect is hiding on the lichen, waiting for darkness?

Living on Lichen

Moths are hiding on the tree stump until it's time to go flying at night.

Can you spot the moth?

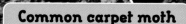

Common carpet moth

Their **camouflage** makes them almost invisible to birds and other **predators** that might eat them.

Some types of moths lay their eggs in the clumps of lichen on the tree stump.

They make sure that when their caterpillars hatch, they are surrounded by their favorite food—lichen!

Brussels lace caterpillar

A Brussels lace caterpillar has camouflage to help it hide from predators among its food.

Lichen

Which little tree stump animal has a clever way to catch flying insects?

23

A Tree Stump Trap

A spider has built a web to trap flies, wasps, moths, and other insects.

She waits with her feet touching long strands of silk attached to her web.

When the strands vibrate, she knows something is trapped!

Spider web

Spider

Wasp

Silk that's made inside the spider's body

The spider's powerful venom will usually kill her prey. Then, juices from the spider's stomach turn the wrapped insect into a liquid snack.

The spider rushes to her struggling **prey** and using her fangs, injects it with **venom**.

The venom stops her meal from moving while she wraps it in silk.

Which legless spider hunter is heading toward the spider's web?

25

When Is a Worm Not a Worm?

At sunset, a slow worm slides from her tree stump hiding place.

She is hunting for spiders, slugs, and snails.

Slow worms may look like snakes, but they are actually legless lizards.

Slow worm

Slug

Slow worm

A slow worm has a clever trick to avoid becoming a bird's supper.

If a bird grabs the slow worm's tail, the end of the tail breaks off—still wriggling!

The slow worm escapes, and in time, its tail will grow back.

Tail

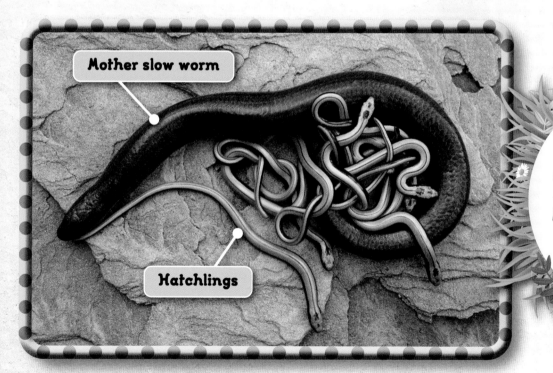

Mother slow worm

Hatchlings

A slow worm's eggs hatch inside her body. Then, she gives birth to tiny hatchlings that are about 1.5 inches (4 cm) long.

Which slim, furry hunter is still looking for food around the tree stump?

Time for Supper!

The weasel didn't catch the wood mouse—this time!

But the fierce little hunter has caught a rabbit, twice her size.

Weasel

Rabbit

Weasel kitten

The weasel has a den of tiny kittens to feed, so she needs to bring home lots of food.

Once the kittens are older, the weasel will bring them live prey so they can learn how to kill.

Weasels eat mice, voles, frogs, rabbits, and birds. They raid birds' nests, too, and eat the eggs.

We may not always see what lives in and around a tree stump.

But day and night, a lot is going on in this microhabitat!

A Tree Stump Food Web

A food web shows who eats who in a habitat.

This food web shows the connections between some of the living things on a tree stump.

Plants and lichen can make the food they need for energy inside themselves. To do this, they need sunlight.

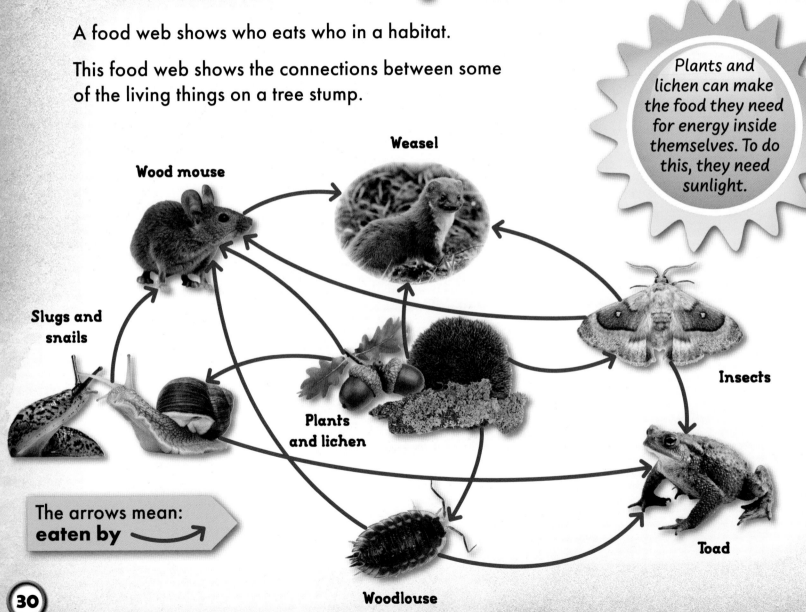

Weasel

Wood mouse

Slugs and snails

Plants and lichen

Insects

Toad

Woodlouse

The arrows mean: **eaten by**

Glossary

algae
Plant-like living things that mostly grow and live in water. Like plants, algae use sunlight to make their own food.

camouflage
Colors, markings, or body parts that help an animal blend into its habitat.

cocoon
A case in which some insects change from a larva into a pupa and then into an adult.

fungi
A group of living things that includes mushrooms, toadstools, and mold.

larva
The young form of some animals. A caterpillar is a type of larva.

leaf litter
Dead plant material, such as leaves and twigs, that has fallen to the ground.

microhabitat
A very small habitat. The word "micro" means very small.

microscopic
Too small to see without a microscope.

nutrients
Substances needed by a plant or animal to help it live and grow.

predator
An animal that hunts and eats other animals.

prey
An animal that is hunted and eaten by other animals.

venom
Poison that is injected into a victim by a bite or sting.

Index

A
ants 7

C
camouflage 22–23
caterpillars 23
centipedes 16

F
ferns 13
fungi 5, 8, 17, 20–21

I
insects 5, 11, 16, 18–19, 22–23, 24–25, 30

L
lichen 20–21, 22–23, 30

M
moss 4–5, 6, 9, 12–13, 14–15, 16, 30
moths 22–23, 24, 30

S
slow worms 26–27
slugs 11, 26, 30
snails 6–7, 26, 30
spiders 16, 24–25, 26
stag beetles 5, 18–19

T
tardigrades 14–15
toads 10–11, 30

W
weasels 7, 28–29, 30
wood mice 7, 8–9, 10, 21, 28–29, 30
woodlice 16–17, 30